W9-CFK-982

Christmas Treasures

Christmas Treasures

By Rubel Shelly   Illustrated by David Arms

BROADMAN & HOLMAN PUBLISHERS

Nashville, Tennessee

© 1998 by Rubel Shelly
All rights reserved
Printed in the United States of America

0-8054-0194-6

Published by Broadman & Holman Publishers, Nashville, Tennessee
Editorial Team: Vicki Crumpton, Janis Whipple, Kim Overcash
Typesetting: TF Designs
Page Design: Paul T. Gant Art & Design

Dewey Decimal Classification: 242
Subject Heading: CHRISTMAS
Library of Congress Card Catalog Number: 98-27842

Unless otherwise stated all Scripture citation is from the NIV, the Holy Bible, New International Version, copyright © 1973, 1978, 1984 by International Bible Society; other versions include *The Message,* the New Testament in Contemporary English, © 1993 by Eugene H. Peterson, published by NavPress, Colorado Springs, Colo., and *The New Century Version*, copyright © 1987 by Worthy Publishing, Fort Worth, Tex., used by permission.

Library of Congress Cataloging-in-Publication Data

Christmas treasures / compiled by Rubel Shelly ; art by David Arms.
    p. cm.
    ISBN 0-8054-0194-6 (hc)
    1. Christmas.   I. Shelly, Rubel, 1945– .
  BV45.C57   1998
  242'.335—dc21

        98-27842
        CIP

1 2 3 4 5 02 01 00 99 98

To the Women in Our Lives

Our Mothers

Jean Arms   Lucille Shelly

Our Wives

Michelle   Myra

Our Daughters

Shelly   Michelle

David Arms   *Richard Shelly*

Lord Jesus, who didst take little children into Thine arms and laugh and play with them, bless, we pray Thee, all children at this Christmastide.

As with shining eyes and glad hearts they nod their heads so widely at the stories of the angels, and a baby cradled in the hay at the end of the way of a wandering star, may their faith and expectation be a rebuke of our own faithlessness. Help us to make this season all joy for them, a time that shall make Thee, Lord Jesus, even more real to them.

—Peter Marshall
The Prayers of Peter Marshall

Author Index

Preface

If there is life on Mars and someone from there comes to Earth during the six weeks leading up to December 25, he/she/it could get terribly confused. Think about it: *What would that creature take the "Christmas message" to be?*

Are these "Holy Days" or "Holidays"?

Is the central character Jesus or Santa?

Is the story about a stable and shepherds or a sleigh and eight tiny reindeer?

Did Wise Men come from the east or was it Frosty who came from the north?

Is the musical message "Fall on your knees" or "Deck the halls"?

Is the personal goal of the season discipleship or salesmanship?

Do the headlines shout "Only a short time until Jesus returns" or "Only a few more shopping days left"?

Did Mary tell the angel "God's will be done" or "Merry Christmas to all and to all a good night"?

Do Christian families worship at their hearths or roast chestnuts on the open fire?

Is the most popular Christmas special *Rudolph the Red-Nosed Reindeer* or *The Life of Christ*?

Is the key to an authentically "wonderful life" Christian faith and discipleship or watching Jimmy Stewart in black and white rather than color?

Is the seasonal issue God's love or Wall Street's bounce?

The people most confused by what we have done with this holiday are more likely to be our own non-Christian neighbors than Martian visitors. Sadly, some of our own children and grandchildren may have the stories so convoluted in their minds that they are mixed up about the meaning of the season too.

We have no control over the way our culture runs the different themes of Christmas together. (Have you seen the "nativity scene" with Santa bowing at the manger?!) We *do* have control over the Christmas cards we select for our friends and the decoration motif we emphasize in our homes. We can invite an unchurched neighbor or friend to a Christmas musical or to worship on the Sunday before Christmas. We can pray at our holiday meals—no matter who the guests are—and thank Jesus for coming to the world to save sinners.

I (Rubel) have been collecting Christmas quotations about the meaning of God's entry into flesh for years. The Incarnation is the primary miracle that makes all the rest of Jesus' signs possible to us. It is proof that "Jesus is not ashamed to call [human beings] brothers" (Heb. 2:11b). "Since the children have flesh and blood, he too shared in their humanity so that by his death he might destroy him who holds the power of death—that is, the devil—and free those who all their lives were held in slavery by their fear of death" (Heb. 2:14-15). But his death and resurrection are impossible without a genuine and complete Incarnation. Each of the quotations in this book can be thought of as someone's line of sight on this wondrous event from which each reader may potentially gain a new insight. Like a diamond catching light by its different facets as it rotates, this book seeks to turn the Christ-event before you so that your fascination with the beauty of God's love may be more complete.

I (David) have tried to provide pieces of contemporary art that bring their own non-verbal insights into play. The artwork is deliberately stark. As I reflect on the Incarnation, I see people standing in a peculiar sort of loneliness within the will of God. Mary is alone as a frightened teenager with a child in her womb. Joseph is left to ponder the meaning of Mary's pregnancy.

With God's explanation given, the little family in Nazareth is alone amidst the gossip of town wags. And Jesus! The Son of God who had become the Son of Man was in "hostile territory" where he would not be received but rejected, not crowned but crucified. Oh, they were very real people. Against the tendency to sentimentalize the Christmas story, I have tried to paint real people in ways that suggest actual, everyday—perhaps even "ordinary"—events. Thus I have portrayed the angel's hand touching Mary in order to take away her fears. I have painted Mary and Joseph walking together with their baby into a lonely landscape. In my own life and family, these are things I witness and experience.

Together we offer you words and pictures designed to point to Jesus. We want our offering of *Christmas Treasures* to enrich your own faith. We hope it will even allow you to share your faith with others. Above all, we want it to give glory to God.

For that theoretical Martian or your real-life family and friends, let there be no ambiguity in what they learn from you about this time of year. May it be clear to them that it is a birthday bash for Jesus rather than a drunken party for an overweight guy who needs a shave.

—Rubel Shelly & David Arms

The Word of God, Jesus Christ, on account of his great love for mankind, became what we are in order to make us what he is himself.

—Irenaeus
Adversus haereses, V

You have come to us as a small child, but you have brought us the greatest of all gifts, the gift of eternal love. Caress us with your tiny hands, embrace us with your tiny arms, and pierce our hearts with your soft, sweet cries.

—Bernard of Clairvaux

It seems, then," said Tirian, . . . "that the Stable seen from within and the Stable seen from without are two different places."

"Yes," said the Lord Digory. "Its inside is bigger than its outside."

"Yes," said Queen Lucy. "In our world too, a Stable once had something inside it that was bigger than our whole world."

—C. S. Lewis
The Last Battle, *Chronicles of Narnia*

Christmas is the gift from heaven
Of God's Son given for free;
If Christmas isn't found in your heart,
You won't find it under the tree.

—Charlotte Carpenter
Herald of Holiness

Meanwhile, the city hums. The merchants are unaware that God has visited their planet. The innkeeper would never believe that he had just sent God into the cold. And the people would scoff at anyone who told them the Messiah lay in the arms of a teenager on the outskirts of their village. They were all too busy to consider the possibility.

Those who missed His Majesty's arrival that night missed it not because of evil acts or malice; no, they missed it because they simply weren't looking.

Little has changed in the last two thousand years, has it?

—Max Lucado
God Came Near

On that first Christmas morning, the world must have seemed a hard place to Mary. At the end of a weary journey there was "no room at the inn."

The only shelter offered to her was the "lowly cattle shed."

I find this a great mystery and a great wonder. Every day science discovers more and more the complex wisdom of God. Anyone who uses his mind has a much bigger idea of God than our grandfathers, or even our fathers, ever had. Yet God has been here on this planet, in person.

What we are celebrating . . . is not the feast of jolly old Father Christmas or good King Wenceslas, or a beautiful fairy tale.

We are celebrating the visit of God.

How marvelous!

—J. B. Phillips
For This Day

My ideal Christmas includes clean snow, warmth, singing, peace, and joy. It has no room for snow splashed with the blood of human suffering. It crowds out nakedness, loneliness, and fear.

How wrong it is to see the unhappy scenes as intrusions, even at Christmas. Instead, they should help us understand what Christmas means. God did not come to a perfect world; he came to one that suffers.

—Randall L. Frame
Christianity Today

Maker of the sun,
He is made under the sun.
In the Father he remains,
From his mother he goes forth.
Creator of heaven and earth,
He was born on earth under heaven.
Unspeakably wise,
He is wisely speechless.
Filling the world,
He lies in a manger.
Ruler of the stars,
He nurses at his mother's bosom.
He is both great in the nature of God,
And small in the form of a servant.

—Augustine

34

Christmas is the most joyful and widely celebrated festival in Christendom. Wherever Christianity has been significant, the birth of Jesus of Nazareth has been a time of rejoicing and gathering to worship this newborn child.... The ideal of self-giving love is in the air, and we give ourselves time to remember those who have tried to give us that kind of caring. The warm, human quality of the Christian holy day still remains. Warring nations declare cease-fire for the day. Families gather together. To most of our society it seems utterly wrong that, at Christmas time, any person should be alone or hungry or any child be without some gifts.

—Morton Kelsey
The Drama of Christmas

There's no reason for any Christian to be a Scrooge about Christmas. The parties, food, trees, and gifts are wonderful—and great fun. They just mustn't be allowed to overshadow the spiritual theme of this special season for Christians.

—Rubel Shelly

Crib and cross: these are the nethermost extremes of life's curve; no man can go any deeper than this; and he traversed it all.

I do not need first to become godly and noble before I can have part in him. For there are no depths in my life where he has not already come to meet me, no depths to which he has not been able to give meaning by surrounding them with love and making them the place where he visits me and brings me back home.

—Helmut Thielicke
Christianity Today

As Joseph looked at Mary, asleep now, he could not keep back the tears. He should have been able to provide something better for her tonight. They had just arrived in the city of David, and there had been no room in the overcrowded inns. That they had even this much sanctuary was due to a stranger's kindness rather than Joseph's ingenuity or ability to provide. . . .

Was Joseph serving the Christ-child that night in ministering to him in an animal shelter? Do we serve him any less when we offer our ministries now? And would he want us to feel guilty that we cannot do more than use the resources he has placed in our hands? I've never done enough for God in any setting, but I'm beginning to understand that my incomplete and imperfect attempts are all he has ever asked.

—Rubel Shelly
What Child Is This?

Bring a torch, Jeannette, Isabella;
Bring a torch, come swiftly and run.
Christ is born, tell the folk of the village;
Jesus is sleeping in His cradle.
Ah, ah, beautiful is the Mother;
Ah, ah, beautiful is her Son.

Hasten now, good folk of the village;
Hasten now, the Christ-Child to see.
You will find Him asleep in the manger;
Quietly come and whisper softly,
Hush, hush, peacefully now He slumbers;
Hush, hush, peacefully now He sleeps.

—Anonymous

39

Not long ago I walked down the corridor of a retirement center, looking at the Christmas decorations that residents had made for their doors. The decorations were small, not complicated or expensive. I guessed that they had been made in some craft session. A few were evident variations on a single pattern. One was very different. It had no tinsel; no colored Christmas seals. It looked more like a place card with just a few decorative pen strokes. It read simply, "Welcome, Lord Jesus."

Decorating for Christmas gives us a wonderful opportunity to open our hearts to Jesus the Christ. As we get out the seasonal paraphernalia, let's make the manger scene an occasion to welcome the Son of God into our home. As we put the Christmas symbols on our tree, let's do it with a prayer for God's presence in our lives.

—H. George Anderson
The Lutheran

It's a tough job trying to make Christmas nonreligious.... To eliminate Christ from Christmas you would have to destroy all the evidence—including the Michelangelos, the Rembrandts, Rubens, and da Vincis, the works of Beethoven, Haydn, Bach, Mozart, and Handel. To search for the millions of Bibles, translated into many languages and distributed around the world, would take quite a force. The job would be too big for the FBI, KGB, and Scotland Yard combined.

—Ruth Hackman
God in the Midst of Every Day

To avoid offending anybody, the schools dropped religion altogether and started singing about the weather. At my son's school, they now hold the winter program in February and sing increasingly non-memorable songs such as "Winter Wonderland," "Frosty the Snowman" and—this is a real song—"Suzy Snowflake," all of which is pretty funny because we live in Miami.

A visitor from another planet might assume that the children belong to the Church of Meteorology.

—Dave Barry
The Chicago Tribune Magazine

I'm not sure anyone can experience what Christmas really means without confronting that sense of lost innocence and the potential for disillusionment the holiday can bring.

Only after we truly face up to Christmas without Santa can we as adults begin to grapple with what Christmas is all about ... God's gift of ultimate hope that our human destiny is something more than a brief, doomed moment in "the benign indifference of the universe."

—Jerry Shin
Charlotte Observer

The Christ-child lay on Mary's lap,
    His hair was like a light.
(O weary, weary is the world,
    But here is all aright.)

The Christ-child lay on Mary's breast,
    His hair was like a star.
(O stern and cunning are the kings,
    But here the true hearts are.)

The Christ-child lay on Mary's heart,
    His hair was like a fire.
(O weary, weary is the world,
    But here the world's desire.)

The Christ-child stood at Mary's knee,
    His hair was like a crown.
And all the flowers looked up at Him,
    And all the stars looked down.

—G. K. Chesterton
The Wild Knight

44

How silently, how silently
The wondrous gift is giv'n!
So God imparts to human hearts
The blessings of his heav'n.
No ear may hear His coming,
But in this world of sin.
Where meek souls will receive Him still
The dear Christ enters in.

—Phillips Brooks
"O Little Town of Bethlehem"

In the super-miracle of the Incarnation, our very Creator, Preserver, Judge, becomes our Kinsman, Sinbearer, Redeemer! Of all miracles and mysteries this is the most staggering.

—J. Sidlow Baxter
Awake, My Heart

What a paradox that a babe in a manger should be called mighty! Yet even as a babe, Jesus Christ was the center of power. His birth affected the heavens and caused a dazzling star to appear. The star aroused the interest of the Magi, and they left their homes and made a long journey to Jerusalem. Their announcement about the newborn king unnerved Herod and his court. Jesus' birth brought angels from heaven and simple shepherds from their flocks on the hillside. Midnight became midday as the glory of the Lord appeared to men.

—Warren W. Wiersbe
The Names of Jesus

The gospel must be culturally contextualized, yet it must "gospelize" the cultural context itself. The incarnation is the ultimate event of contextualization. This means that the gospel remains a stumbling block and no contextualization can domesticate it.

—Shoki Coe, quoted in
Christian Century

Mary and Joseph, along with both the simple shepherds and the learned Wise Men, show us that communication with the Lord needs two partners: God sends a message, but we must be willing to receive the news.

—Christopher M. Belitto
U.S. Catholic

The Word had become flesh: a real human baby. He had not ceased to be God; He was no less God then than before; but He had begun to be man. He was not now God *minus* some elements of His deity, but God *plus* all that He had made His own by taking manhood to himself.

—J. I. Packer
Knowing God

50

He undertook to help the descendants of Abraham, fashioning a body for himself from a woman and sharing our flesh and blood, to enable us to see in him not only God, but also, by reason of this union, a man like ourselves.

—Cyril of Alexandria

Jesus—a simple name with so much power and meaning, but on that night so long ago, a tiny baby, wrapped by Mary in swaddling clothes, waving little arms, hungrily sucking a fist, was like any other newborn baby.

He was helpless and dependent, and Mary was His hope of survival, His nourishment, His very lifeline. God entrusted His most priceless gift to a very human, very young, earthly mother. Why?

Because God so loved—that He gave. He relinquished His hold on His Son and placed Him in fragile human arms.

—Janette Oke
Reflections on the Christmas Story

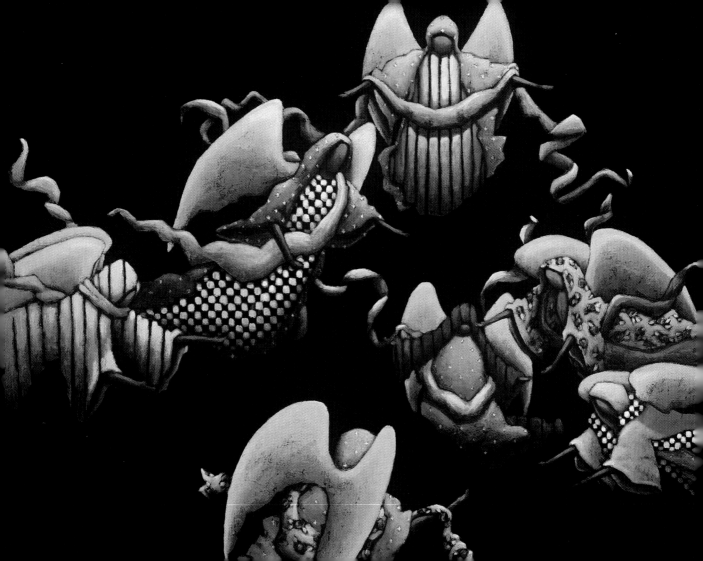

The implications of the name *Immanuel* are both comforting and unsettling. Comforting, because He has come to share the danger as well as the drudgery of our everyday lives. He desires to weep with us and to wipe away our tears. And what seems most bizarre, Jesus Christ, the Son of God, longs to share in and to be the source of the laughter and the joy we all too rarely know.

—Michael Card
Immanuel

The stunning point of Christmas is that God considered my needs and the worth of my relationship to Him to be sufficient cause to go through the trauma of changing places.

—Joseph M. Stowell
Moody Monthly

The Son of God became man to enable men to become the sons of God.

—C. S. Lewis
Mere Christianity

It was to simple men of the fields that God's message first came. But these shepherds were in all likelihood very special shepherds. . . . It is most likely that these shepherds were in charge of the flocks from which the Temple offerings were chosen. It is a lovely thought that the shepherds who looked after the Temple lambs were the first to see the Lamb of God who takes away the sin of the world.

—William Barclay
The Daily Study Bible: Luke

Just as Our Lord came into human history from outside, so He must come into me from outside. Have I allowed my personal human life to become a "Bethlehem" for the Son of God?

—Oswald Chambers
My Utmost for His Highest

Lord Jesus, may your light shine upon our way;
as once it guided the steps of the magi:
that we too may be led into your presence
and worship you,
the Child of Mary,
the Word of the Father,
the King of nations,
the Savior of mankind;
to whom be glory for ever.

—Frank Colquhoun
The Complete Book of Christian Prayer

O Sovereign God! You have humbled yourself in order to exalt us. You became poor so that we might become rich. You came to us so that we can come to you. You took upon yourself our humanity in order to raise us up into eternal life. All this comes through your grace, free and unmerited; all this through your beloved Son, our Lord and Savior, Jesus Christ.

—Karl Barth
Prayer

If you look, you'll see Him. The spirit of Christ is everywhere during the holidays. That's why we love this time of year so much. . . .

His spirit is there in the bell ringers, soup-kitchen servers, carolers, and helpers of the homeless.

He's right there in the bright smile of an expectant child, the tears of a proud mother, and the embrace between longing parents and a prodigal son or daughter who's been called home by a still small voice.

And when you look into a mirror, don't be surprised if you see the sparkle of His spirit staring back at you.

—John William Smith
Hugs for the Holidays

We live in a spiritually troubled time in history. Christianity has gone over to the jingle-bell crowd. Everyone is just delighted that Jesus has to do all of the sorrowing, all of the suffering, all of the dying.

—A. W. Tozer
Men Who Met God

Come, thou long-expected Jesus,
Born to set thy people free;
From our fears and sins release us;
Let us find our rest in thee.
Israel's strength and consolation,
Hope of all the earth thou art;
Dear desire of every nation,
Joy of every longing heart.

Born thy people to deliver,
Born a child and yet a King,
Born to reign in us forever,
Now thy gracious kingdom bring.
By thine own eternal spirit
Rule in all our hearts alone,
By thine all sufficient merit,
Raise us to thy glorious throne.

—Charles Wesley

The true Christian religion ... does not begin at the top, as all other religions do; it begins at the bottom. You must run directly to the manger and the mother's womb, embrace this Infant and Virgin's Child in your arms and look at Him—born, being nursed, growing up, going about in human society, teaching, dying, rising again, ascending above all the heavens, and having authority over all things.

—Martin Luther
Lectures on Galatians

Christmas has absolutely destroyed [the real] understanding of the Good News. It's trained people to believe that Christmas is fundamentally about giving and receiving and that our happiness is in giving and getting what we want. But, in fact, the best Christmases are often the ones in which one doesn't get what one wants.

—Stanley Hauerwas, quoted in
U.S. Catholic

When Joseph came home with word of the census and explained the trip that was involved, I wonder if Mary cried? Did they both cry?

As they made the journey, do you think they knew what lay ahead? Might they have feared running into thieves along the road? Is it possible that they felt forsaken when the only shelter they could find in Bethlehem was a stable? Were they frightened when Mary went into labor?

So many things just don't seem to fit with the storybook image we perpetuate about Joseph and Mary. Isn't it better to see them as real people? They were people like us who had to deal with daily realities without understanding their ultimate significance.

—Rubel Shelly
What Child Is This?

Everywhere, everywhere, Christmas tonight!
Christmas in lands of the fir-tree and pine,
Christmas in lands of the palm-tree and vine,
Christmas where snow peaks stand solemn and white,
Christmas where cornfields stand sunny and bright.
Christmas where children are hopeful and gay,
Christmas where old men are patient and gray,
Christmas where peace, like a dove in his flight,
Broods o'er brave men in the thick of the fight;
Everywhere, everywhere, Christmas tonight!

For the Christ-child who comes is the Master of all;
No palace too great, no cottage too small.

—Phillips Brooks
"Christmas Everywhere"

Loving Father, help us remember the birth of Jesus, that we may share in the song of the angels, the gladness of the shepherds, and the wisdom of the wise men.

Close the door of hate and open the door of love all over the world.

Let kindness come with every gift and good desires with every greeting.

Deliver us from evil by the blessing which Christ brings, and teach us to be merry with clean hearts.

May the Christmas morning make us happy to be thy children, and the Christmas evening bring us to our beds with grateful thoughts, forgiving and forgiven, for Jesus' sake. Amen.

—Robert Louis Stevenson

Christmas for millions is just "the holiday season." Are we losing the sense of marvel at the Christmas miracle?

Why, this is the most stupendous and astonishing wonder which could ever engross the human mind—that the eternal, infinite Creator of the universe should enter our human life, and assume our human nature, by being born as a baby of a human mother!

—J. Sidlow Baxter
Awake, My Heart

We know from Scripture that Jesus wept as a man. It is naive to think He did not cry as a baby. Tears are a basic part of what it means to be human. It is one of the sad signs of our fallen world that the first sign we give to show that we're alive is a cry.

It was to this fallen world that Jesus came, not an imaginary one without tears. For the "Man of Sorrows" it would seem that tears were an even more integral part of His life than ours. He came as much to weep for us as to die for us.

—Michael Card
Immanuel

T he Word was made flesh" (John 1:1 4); God became man; the divine Son became a Jew; the Almighty appeared on earth as a helpless human baby, unable to do more than lie and stare and wriggle and make noises, needing to be fed and changed and taught to talk like any other child. And there was no illusion or deception in this: the babyhood of the Son of God was a reality. The more you think about it, the more staggering it gets. Nothing in fiction is so fantastic as is this truth of the incarnation.

—J. I. Packer
Knowing God

What we do better indicates what we believe than what we say, and too many of us focus most of our attention on the worldly and ephemeral. Jesus calls us to remember that the true significance of our lives lies not in our worldly fame or appearance or in the splash we make in the social whirl, or even in our correct statements of dogma, but in how much our actions reflect the love expressed in Jesus Christ.

At the first Christmas, God slipped into our world in a humble stable to give us a new way to value the importance of what we do and are.

—Morton Kelsey
The Drama of Christmas

That night when in the Judean skies
      The mystic star dispensed its light,
A blind man moved in his sleep—
      And dreamed that he had sight.

That night when shepherds heard the song
      Of angelic choiring near,
A deaf man stirred in slumber's spell—
      And dreamed that he could hear!

That night when in the cattle stall
      Slept Child and mother cheek by jowl,
A cripple turned his twisted limbs—
      And dreamed that he was whole.

That night when o'er the newborn Babe
      The tender Mary rose to lean,
A loathsome leper smiled in sleep—
      And dreamed that he was clean.

That night when to the mother's breast
      The little King was held secure,
A harlot slept a happy sleep—
      And dreamed that she was pure!

That night when in the manger lay
      The Sanctified who came to save,
A man moved in the sleep of death—
      And dreamed there was no grave.

—Anonymous

Our trouble is we want the peace without the Prince.

—Addison Leitch
Christianity Today

Millions of perfectly healthy and worthy men and women still keep Christmas; and do in all sincerity keep it holy as well as happy. But there are some, profiting by such natural schemes of play and pleasure-seeking, who have used it for things far baser than either pleasure-seeking or play. They have betrayed Christmas. For them the substance of Christmas, like the substance of Christmas pudding, has become stale stuff in which their own treasure is buried; and they have only multiplied the sixpences into thirty pieces of silver.

—G. K. Chesterton
Illustrated London News

The innkeeper who gave Mary and Joseph a Christmas Eve cave should be a holiday model for Christians as they celebrate the birth of the Messiah. That's because that Middle Eastern Howard Johnson had the simple consideration to think beyond the "no" that could have easily been his complete conversation with the visiting strangers who came to his door.

In contrast, many Christians who honor the child born that night say no all the time to strangers during the very time of year when they should be opening their doors to the lonely, forgotten, and alienated.

—James Breig
U.S. Catholic

Jesus Christ founded His Kingdom on the weakest link of all—a Baby.

—Oswald Chambers
Shade of His Hand

Not of flesh and blood the Son,
Offspring of the Holy One;
Born of Mary ever blest,
God in flesh is manifest.

Wondrous birth, O wondrous child,
Of the Virgin undefiled,
Though by all the world disowned,
Still to be in heaven enthroned.

—Ambrose of Milan

Once it happened, once in the world's history it happened, that someone came forward with the claim that he was the Son of God and the assertion "I and the Father are one," and that he proved the legitimacy of that claim, not by acting like a supernatural being or stunning men with his wisdom or communicating knowledge of higher worlds, but rather by proving his claim through the depths to which he descended.

A Son of God who defends his title with the arguments that he is the brother of even the poorest and the guilty and takes their burden upon himself; this is a fact one can only note, and shake one's head in unbelief—or one must worship and adore. There is no other alternative.

I must worship. That's why I celebrate Christmas.

—Helmut Thielicke
Christianity Today

All praise to Thee, Eternal Lord,
Clothed in a garb of flesh and blood;
Choosing a manger for a throne,
While worlds on worlds are Thine alone.

—Martin Luther

He came to save all through his own person; all, that is, who through him are reborn to God; infants, children, boys, young men and old. Therefore he passed through every stage of life. He was made an infant for infants, sanctifying infancy; a child among children, sanctifying childhood, and setting an example of filial affection, of righteousness and obedience; a young man among young men, becoming an example to them, and sanctifying them to the Lord.

—Irenaeus

How proper it is that Christmas should follow Advent. For him who looks toward the future, the Manger is situated on Golgotha, and the Cross has already been raised in Bethlehem.

—Dag Hammarskjold
Markings

The Christmas spirit does not shine out in the Christian snob. For the Christmas spirit is the spirit of those who, like their Master, live their whole lives on the principle of making themselves poor—spending and being spent—to enrich their fellowmen, giving time, trouble, care and concern, to do good to others—and not just their own friends—in whatever way there seems need.

—J. I. Packer
Knowing God

J esus on His Mother's breast
In the stable cold,
Spotless Lamb of God was He,
Shepherd of the fold.
Let us kneel with Mary Maid,
With Joseph bent and hoary,
With saint and angel, ox and ass,
To hail the King of Glory.

—Christina Rossetti
Christmas Daybreak

When a ray is projected from the sun, it is a portion of the whole sun; but the sun will be in the ray because it is a ray of the sun; the substance is not separated but extended. So from spirit comes spirit, and God from God, as light is kindled from light. . . .

This ray of God . . . glided down into a virgin, in her womb was fashioned as flesh, is born as man mixed with God. The flesh was built up by the spirit, was nourished, grew up, spoke, taught, worked, and was Christ.

—Tertullian
Apology

Have we ... reduced the stable scene to some cutesy little scenario that has no meaning left in it at all? Have we lost the sense of awe that there, in that stable, *God became man?*

What can be the point of Christmas if it is here today and gone tomorrow? For all our celebrations this time of year, why do so many fail to recognize Christmas's Lord?

—Rick Mylander
Covenant Companion

Yesterday, coming home from a crowded airline flight, my attention was captured by a young mother and her baby boy. How fragile, how absolutely dependent for survival he was, and how marvelous. Studying him, thinking about his promise and his hope for the future, I could not escape the fact that God became just like him.

As always, I was uncomfortable with the thought, as I am uncomfortable with all the other truths of my faith that hang on this central mystery of God's love saving us from inside our own flesh and bone, nerve and muscle, mind and heart.

—Mary Evelyn Jegen
How You Can Be a Peacemaker

When Jesus is with us, all is well, and nothing seems hard; but when Jesus is absent, everything is difficult. When Jesus does not speak to the heart, all other comfort is unavailing; but if Jesus speaks but a single word, we are greatly comforted....

What can the world offer you, without Jesus? ... Poorest of all men is he who lives without Jesus, and richest of all is he who stands in favor with Jesus.

—Thomas à Kempis
The Imitation of Christ

Christmas does not deny sorrow its place in the world. But the message of Christmas is that joy is bigger than despair, that peace will outlast turmoil, that love has crushed all the evil, hatred, and pain the world at its worst can muster.

—Randall L. Frame
Christianity Today

Be humble and a man of peace, and Jesus will abide with you. But if you turn aside to worldly things, you will soon cause Jesus to leave you, and you will lose his grace. And if you drive him away and lose him, with whom may you take refuge, and whom will you seek for your friend?

Without a friend you cannot live happily, and if Jesus is not your best friend, you will be exceedingly sad and lonely; so it is foolish to trust or delight in any other.

It is better to have the whole world as your enemy, than offend Jesus. Therefore, of all dear friends, let Jesus be loved first and above all.

Love all men for Jesus' sake, but Jesus for himself.

—Thomas à Kempis
The Imitation of Christ

I love Luther's suggestion that the humble dwelling was probably a great trial to the Magi. Had they come thousands of miles to this—a poor peasant's home outside the big city? It is a credit to their faith that they went in.

—Kent R. Hughes
Christianity Today

The fact remains that our world never comes as close to being in contact with its greatest hope as it is at Christmas.

—Rick Mylander
Covenant Companion

He was born in an obscure village, the child of a peasant woman.

He grew up in still another village, where he worked in a carpenter's shop until he was thirty. Then for three years he was an itinerant preacher.

He never wrote a book. He never held an office. He never had a family or owned a house. He did not go to college. He never visited a big city. He never traveled two hundred miles from the place where he was born. He did none of the things one usually associates with greatness.

He had no credentials but himself.

He was only thirty-three when the tide of public opinion turned against him. His friends ran away. He was turned over to his enemies and went through the mockery of a trial. He was nailed to a cross between two thieves. While he was dying, his executioners gambled for his clothing, the only property he had on earth. When he was dead, he was laid in a borrowed grave through the pity of a friend.

Nineteen centuries have come and gone, and today he remains the central figure of the human race, and the leader of mankind's progress. All the armies that ever marched, all the navies that ever sailed, all the parliaments that ever sat, all the kings that ever reigned put together, have not affected the life of man on this planet so much as that one solitary life.

—Anonymous

Nations have their red-letter days, their carnivals and festivals. But once in the year, and only once, the whole world stands still to celebrate the advent of a life.

Only Jesus of Nazareth claims this world-wide, undying remembrance.

You cannot cut Christmas out of the calendar, nor out of the heart of the world.

—Unknown

I often think: "A life is like a day; it goes by so fast. If I am so careless with my days, how can I be careful with my life?"

I know that somehow I have not fully come to believe that urgent things can wait while I attend to what is truly important. It finally boils down to a question of deep and strong conviction.

Once I am truly convinced that preparing the heart is more important than preparing the Christmas tree, I will be a lot less frustrated at the end of a day.

—Henri J. M. Nouwen
New Oxford Review

It is a message of joy and happiness as the whole Christian world celebrates the birth of our savior, Jesus Christ.

We celebrate the day when the Son of God became the Son of Man. We celebrate the day when the Son of the Highest stooped to the lowest, a day when the King of Glory shed his splendor and became poor that we through his poverty might be rich....

Christmas is and should be, the happiest, most joyful time of the year.

—Arthur M. Brazier
*In Our Own Words: A Treasury of Quotations
from the African-American Community*

Paul tells us that it is the world's very wisdom which places it in the gravest danger because that wisdom has no category by which it can interpret the scandalous overture of God. The paradox is that it was the foolish, the poor, the childlike, who somehow found the freshness, the openness to recognize the One who had come, while everyone else busily tried to interpret him away: "Is not this Joseph's son?"

—Richard Holloway
Beyond Belief

Christmas is the gift of God's love. Let us be inspired to give a little of our own.

—Kenneth B. Smith
*In Our Own Words: A Treasury of Quotations
from the African-American Community*

Many of us have found our sensitivities insulted and our convictions offended as court rulings removed the creches from the lawns of our city halls. It's far easier to object to that swipe of secularism than to realize that for years many of us have been living through the Christmas season with, figuratively, no creche on the front lawn of our lives. Caught up in the swirl and storm of the holiday, who of us has taken the time to proclaim Jesus as the reason for the season?

—Joseph M. Stowell
Moody Monthly

Praise God for Christmas.
Praise Him for the Incarnation, for the Word made
Flesh.
I will not sing of shepherds watching flocks on
frosty night or
angel choristers.
I will not sing of stable bare in Bethlehem,
or lowing oxen,
wise men trailing distant star with
gold, frankincense and myrrh.

Tonight I will sing praise to the
Father who stood on heaven's
threshold and said farewell to
His Son as He stepped across the stars to
Bethlehem and Jerusalem.
And I will sing praise to the infinite eternal Son who
became most finite, a Baby who would one day
be executed for my crimes.
Praise Him in the heavens,
praise Him in the stable,
praise Him in my heart.

—Joseph Bayly
Psalms of My Life

For the essence of sin is man substituting himself for God, while the essence of salvation is God substituting himself for man. Man asserts himself against God and puts himself where only God deserves to be; God sacrifices himself for man and puts himself where only man deserves to be. Man claims prerogatives which belong to God alone; God accepts penalties which belong to man alone.

—John R. W. Stott
The Cross of Christ

From the view of the historians of that time or from a strictly materialistic point of view, it would be mad to compare the stature and significance of these two, Augustus and Jesus of Nazareth. From either point of view there could be no ground for even bringing the man of Nazareth into the August presence of the mighty emperor—even as an academic exercise. As a matter of fact, only one of the Roman historians of that time even mentions Jesus.

Yet the truth is this, the bald historical truth: the only reason most people today have ever heard of Augustus Caesar is that he was part of the historical background for the birth of Jesus of Nazareth.

—Morton Kelsey
The Drama of Christmas

Who would have had sufficient daring of imagination to conceive that God Almighty would have appeared among men as a little child?

We should have conceived something sensational, phenomenal, catastrophic, appalling! The most awful of the natural elements would have formed His retinue, and men would be chilled and frozen with fear.

But He came as a little child. The great God "emptied Himself"; He let in the light as our eyes were able to bear it.

—John Henry Jowett
My Daily Meditation

Jesus, the Christ, is the Eternal One, for in the fullness of time He humbled Himself. John's description is plain: the Word was made flesh and dwelt among us.

I confess I would have liked to have seen the baby Jesus. But the glorified Jesus yonder at the right hand of the Majesty on high, was the baby Jesus once cradled in the manger straw. Taking a body of humiliation, He was still the Creator who made the wood of that manger, [and] made the straw.

—A. W. Tozer
Renewed Day by Day

Beyond all question, the mystery of godliness is great:

He appeared in a body,
was vindicated by the Spirit,
was seen by angels,
was preached among the nations,
was believed on in the world,
was taken up in glory.

— 1 Timothy 3:16

Consistent with the secular dictates of our culture, Christmas has become an exercise in excess. Too much money spent. Too much debt accumulated. Too much alcohol. Too much food. Too much stress. Too much of everything except the one we say the holiday celebrates.

—Rubel Shelly

At that time, Augustus Caesar sent an order to all people in the countries that were under Roman rule. The order said that they must list their names in a register. This was the first registration taken while Quirinius was governor of Syria. And everyone went to their own towns to be registered.

So Joseph left Nazareth, a town in Galilee, and went to the town of Bethlehem in Judea. This town was known as the town of David. Joseph went there because he was from the family of David. Joseph registered with Mary because she was engaged to marry him. (Mary was now pregnant.) While Joseph and Mary were in Bethlehem, the time came for her to have the baby. She gave birth to her first son. There were no rooms left in the inn. So she wrapped the baby with cloths and laid him in a box where animals are fed.

—Luke 2:1-7
The New Century Version

The Christ child is the real model of this "littleness," this poverty, this nothingness. And yet He was All.

God lacked nothing, but there was just one thing He did not have, did not know about: littleness, weakness. He wanted to experience it in Jesus and there, right there, He showed us the right relationship between creature and Creator.

—Carlo Carretto
Letters to Dolcidia

Lord, the calendar calls for Christmas. We have traveled this way before. During this Advent season we would see what we have never seen before, accept what we have refused to think, and hear what we need to understand. Be with us in our goings that we may meet you in your coming. Astonish us until we sing "Glory!" and then enable us to live it out with love and peace. In the name of your Incarnate Word, even Jesus Christ. *Amen.*

—Donald J. Shelby
The Unsettling Season

The world is the place where we meet God because it is the place where God meets us in the person of Jesus Christ.

Christ did not merely inhabit human flesh; he became flesh. He made himself, as God, to be one with humanity in the concrete, historical realities of human life.

Truly, God has entered into the world and it is in the world that Christians must turn to find God.

—James Finley
Merton's Palace of Nowhere

For me, Christmas is memories. It is the smell of spice cake as I walk through the front door of my grandmother's house. It is putting up a Christmas tree in our house—a real tree. It is putting rows and rows of lights—including my personal favorites, bubble lights—all around it.

Christmas is going through the Sears "wish book" with my dad. He was incredibly patient in early December as I found at least three things per page I wanted. The list narrowed toward the Big Day. And there was always just the perfect gift under the tree.

But I wonder about the Christmas memories in the throne room of God. For heaven, Christmas is one member of the family taking leave of home. It is an empty seat that no one can fill until he returns. It is joy mixed with sadness. The joy comes from the knowledge of what is being done for humankind; the sadness lies in the fact that the reaction to it all is known in advance.

From heaven's perspective, it is knowing what Mary, shepherds, and even "wise" men could not know in those earliest days. It is knowing that the cradle leads inevitably to a cross. It is knowing that the cross will become the only hope of salvation for the human race.

Christmas is memories. And it is remembering to remember.

—Rubel Shelly

Acknowledgments

Grateful acknowledgment is made to the following authors and publishers for permission to reproduce copyrighted materials.

H. George Anderson: From *The Lutheran* (Dec. 1997). Copyright © 1997 Augsburg Fortress. Used by permission.

William Barclay: From *Luke: Daily Study Bible Series.* Copyright © 1953. Used by permission of Westminster John Knox Press.

Dave Barry: From "Notes on Western Civilization" in *The Chicago Tribune Magazine* (28 July 1991). Copyright © 1991 The Chicago Tribune.

Karl Barth: From *Prayer.* Copyright © 1952, 1985. Used by permission of Westminster John Knox Press.

J. Sidlow Baxter: *From Awake, My Heart.* Copyright © Kregel Publications. Used by permission.

Joseph Bayly: From *Psalms of My Life.* Copyright © 1992 Chariot Victor Publishing. Used by permission.

Christopher M. Belitto: Reprinted from *U.S. Catholic* (Dec. 1994). Copyright © 1994 Claretian Publications, 205 W. Monroe Street, Chicago, IL 60606. Used by permission.

Jan Berry: From *The Complete Book of Christian Prayer.* Copyright © 1995 SPCK. Used by permission of The Continuum Publishing Company.

Arthur M. Brazier: From *In Our Own Words: A Treasury of Quotations from the African-American Community.* Copyright © 1996 by Elza Dinwiddie-Boyd.

James Breig: Reprinted from *U.S. Catholic* (Dec. 1986). Copyright © 1986 Claretian Publications, 205 W. Monroe Street, Chicago, IL 60606. Used by permission.

Michael Card: From *Immanuel.* Copyright © 1990 by Michael Card. Used by permission of Thomas Nelson Publishers, Nashville, TN.

Charlotte Carpenter: From *Herald of Holiness* (15 Dec. 1982). Copyright © 1982 Herald of Holiness. Used by permission.

Carlo Carretto: From *The God Who Comes* and *Letters to Dolcidia.* Copyright © Orbis Books, Maryknoll, New York. Used by permission.

Oswald Chambers: From *My Utmost for His Highest.* Copyright © 1935 by Dodd Mead & Co., renewed © 1963 by the Oswald Chambers Publications Assn. Ltd. and used by permission of Discovery House Publishers, Box 3566, Grand Rapids, MI 49501. All rights reserved.

Oswald Chambers: From *Shade of His Hand.* Copyright © 1936, 1991 by the Oswald Chambers Publications Assn. Ltd. and used by permission of Discovery House Publishers, Box 3566, Grand Rapids, MI 49501. All rights reserved.

Sallie Chesham: From *WindChimes.* Copyright © Salvation Army Supplies. Used by permission.

G. K. Chesterton: From *The Wild Knight.* Copyright © Ignatius Press, P.O. Box 1339, Fort Collins, CO 80522.

Frank Colquhoun: From *The Complete Book of Christian Prayer.* Copyright © 1995 SPCK. Used by permission of The Continuum Publishing Company.

Catherine de Hueck Doherty: From *Soul of My Soul.* Copyright © 1985 Madonna House Publications. Used by permission.

Father Henry Fehren: Reprinted from *U.S. Catholic* (Dec. 1985). Copyright © 1985 Claretian Publications, 205 W. Monroe Street, Chicago, IL 60606. Used by permission.

James Finley: From *Merton's Palace of Nowhere*. Copyright © 1980 by Ave Maria Press, Notre Dame, IN 46556. Used with permission of the publisher.

Randall L. Frame: From *Christianity Today* (13 Dec. 1985). Copyright © 1985 Christianity Today. Used by permission.

Ruth Hackman: From *God in the Midst of Every Day*. Copyright © 1986 by Augsburg Fortress Publishing Company. Used by permission.

Dag Hammarskjold: From *Markings*. Copyright © 1966 Random House, Inc., New York. Used by permission.

Stanley Hauerwas: Reprinted from an interview in *U.S. Catholic* (June 1991). Copyright © 1991 Claretian Publications, 205 W. Monroe Street, Chicago, IL 60606. Used by permission of the publisher.

Richard Holloway: From *Beyond Belief*. Copyright © 1981 Wm. B. Eerdmans Publishing Company. Used by permission.

Kent R. Hughes: From *Christianity Today* (13 Dec. 1985). Copyright © 1985 Christianity Today. Used by permission.

Mary Evelyn Jegen: From *How You Can Be a Peacemaker*. Copyright © 1985 Ligouri Publications. Used by permission of the author.

Morton Kelsey: From *The Drama of Christmas*. Copyright © 1994 Morton Kelsey. Published by Westminster John Knox Press.

Thomas á Kempis: From *The Imitation of Christ*. Copyright © Ave Maria Press, Notre Dame, IN 46556. Used with permission of the publisher.

Kosuke Koyama: From "Christ's Homelessness" in *Christian Century* (14–21 July 1993). Copyright © 1993 Christian Century Foundation. Used by permission.

Addison Leitch: From *Christianity Today* (22 Dec. 1972). Copyright © 1972 Christianity Today. Used by permission.

C. S. Lewis: From *Mere Christianity* and *Chronicles of Narnia*. Copyright © HarperCollins Publishers Ltd., London, England. Used by permission.

Max Lucado: Excerpted from *God Came Near*. Copyright © 1987 by Max Lucado. Used by permission of Multnomah Publishers, Inc.

Martin Luther: From *Luther's Works*, Vol. 26. Copyright © 1963, 1991 Concordia Publishing House. Used with permission.

Peter Marshall: From The Prayers of Peter Marshall. Copyright 1949, 1950, 1951, and 1954 by Catherine Marshall.

The Message. Copyright © 1994 by Eugene H. Peterson. Published by NavPress Publishing Group, P.O. Box 35001, Colorado Springs, CO 80935

Leon Morris: Reprinted from *The Lord from Heaven*. Copyright © 1974 by InterVarsity Press. Used by permission of the author.

Rick Mylander: From *The Covenant Companion* (Dec. 1988). Copyright © 1988 The Covenant Companion. Used by permission of the author.

The New Century Version. Copyright © 1987 by Worthy Publishing, Fort Worth, TX 76137. Used by permission.

Henri J. M. Nouwen. From *The New Oxford Review* (Nov. 1986). Copyright © 1986 Historical Society of the Episcopal Church, Austin, TX 78705.

Janette Oke: From *Reflections on the Christmas Story*. Copyright © Bethany House Publishers. Used by permission.

Stephen Orchard: From *The Complete Book of Christian Prayer*. Copyright © 1995 SPCK. Used by permission of The Continuum Publishing Company.

J. I. Packer: Reprinted from *Knowing God*. Copyright © 1973 by J. I. Packer. Used by permission from InterVarsity Press, P.O. Box 1400, Downers Grove, IL 60515.

Pope John Paul II: From *Lift up Your Hearts*. Copyright © 1995 Servant Publications, Ann Arbor, MI 48107. Used by permission.

J. B. Phillips: From *For This Day*. Copyright © 1985 Word Books.

Laura B. Randolph: From *In Our Own Words: A Treasury of Quotations from the African-American Community*. Copyright © 1996 by Elza Dinwiddie-Boyd.

Ron Rose: From *Diary of God*. Copyright © 1997 by Ron Rose. Used by permission of Multnomah Publishers, Inc.

Donald J. Shelby: From *The Unsettling Season*. Copyright © 1989 by Donald J. Shelby. Used by permission of Upper Room Books.

Rubel Shelly: From *What Child Is This?* Copyright © 1992 by Howard Publishing Company, West Monroe, LA. Used by permission.

J. Barrie Shepherd: From *A Child Is Born*. Copyright © 1998 J. Barrie Shepherd. Used by permission of Westminster John Knox Press.

Jerry Shin: Reprinted with permission from *The Charlotte Observer*. First published on Dec. 22, 1986. Copyright © 1986 by The Charlotte Observer.

John William Smith: Reprinted from *Hugs for the Holidays*. Copyright © 1997 by Howard Publishing Company, West Monroe, LA. Used by permission.

Kenneth B. Smith: From *In Our Own Words: A Treasury of Quotations from the African-American Community*. Copyright © 1996 by Elza Dinwiddie-Boyd.

R. Eugene Sterner: Reprinted from *Vital Christianity* (14 Dec. 1975). Copyright © Warner Press, Inc., Anderson, Indiana. Used by permission.

John R. W. Stott: Reprinted from *The Authentic Jesus*. Copyright © 1985 by John R. W. Stott. Used by permission of the author.

John R. W. Stott: Reprinted from *The Cross of Christ*. Copyright © 1986 by John R. W. Stott. Used by permission from InterVarsity Press, P.O. Box 1400, Downers Grove, IL 60515.

Joseph M. Stowell: From *Moody Monthly* (Dec. 1989 and Dec. 1992). Copyright © 1989, 1992 Moody Monthly. Used by permission.

Helmut Thielicke: From *Christianity Today* (9 Dec. 1988). Copyright © 1988 Christianity Today. Used by permission.

A. W. Tozer: From *Men Who Met God* and *Renewed Day by Day*. Copyright © Christian Publications, Inc., Camp Hill, PA. Used by permission.

Edgar R. Trexler: From *The Lutheran* (Dec. 1996). Copyright © 1996 Augsburg Fortress. Used by permission.

Desmond Tutu: From *International Christian Digest* (March 1989). Copyright © 1989 The United Methodist Publishing House. Used by permission of the publisher.

C. John Weborg: Excerpt originally appeared in *The Covenant Companion* (Dec. 1994). Copyright © 1994 The Covenant Companion. Used by permission.

Warren W. Wiersbe: From *The Names of Jesus*. Copyright © 1997 by Baker Book House, Grand Rapids, MI. Used by permission of the author.

Every effort has been made to trace and acknowledge copyright holders of all the materials included in this book. For any errors or omissions, we apologize, ask that you notify us with correct information, and pledge to make corrections in any future editions.